POEM ON MARRIAGE

Bahareh Amidi

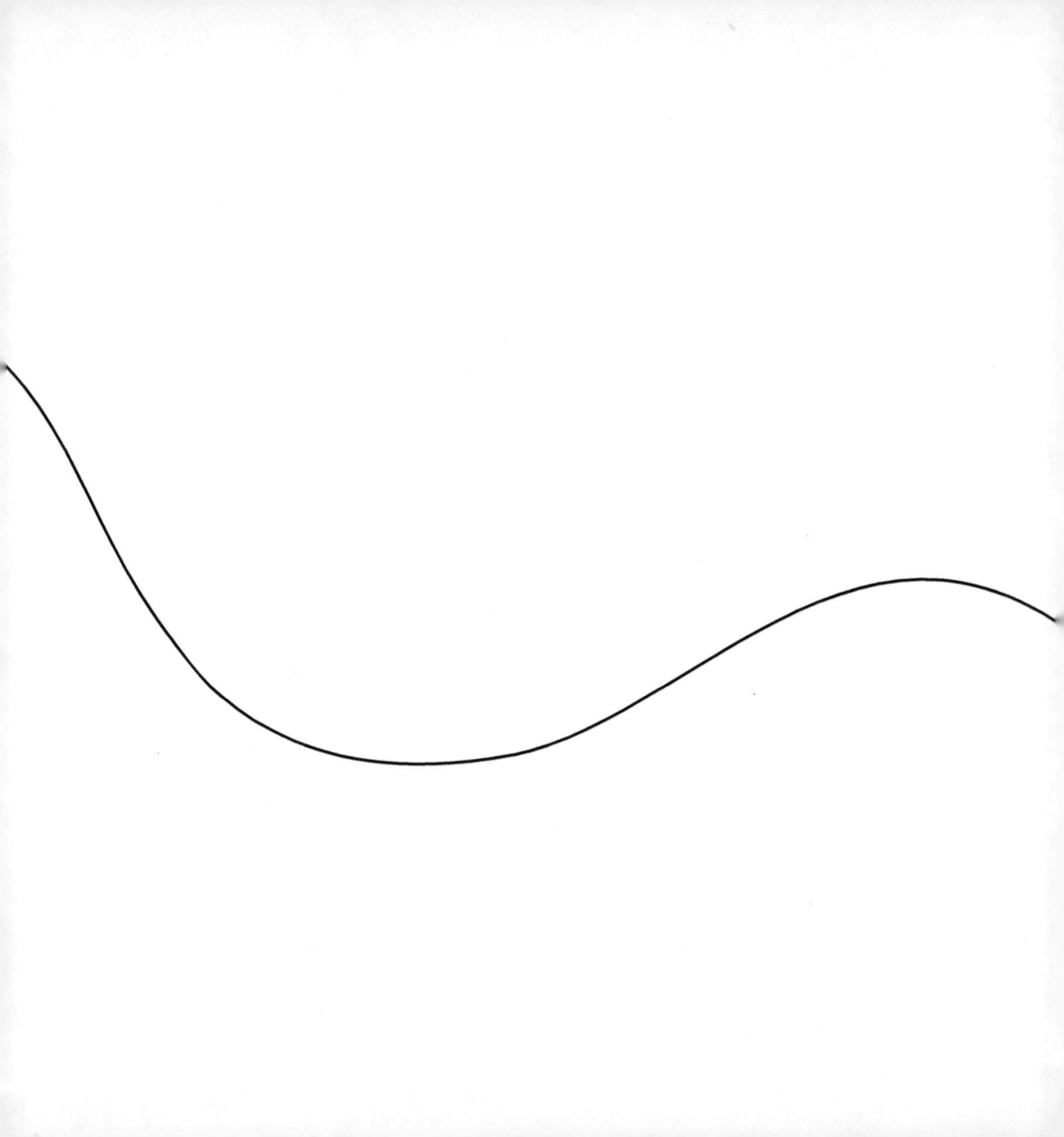

Poem on Marriage

Bahareh

cover and interior illustrations by
   Adora:
    @AdoraArts

email: connect@bahareh.com
facebook.com/Bahareh.Amidi
twitter.com/BaharehAmidi
youtube.com/baharehLIVE
instagram.com/bahareh_poetess
www.bahareh.com

"Let there be spaces in your togetherness."
- Khalil Gibran

Listen to Poem on Marriage

I thought for a while
before I took my pen in hand
and blessed the pages with my thoughts
about marriage and wedding vows.
In my years I have witnessed marriages
that have been nothing
but boredom and disrespect for the other's being.
I have also had the great fortune
of witnessing marriages
that have been like two separate people
wearing each other on their shoulders as pins.
No weight only company and good will.

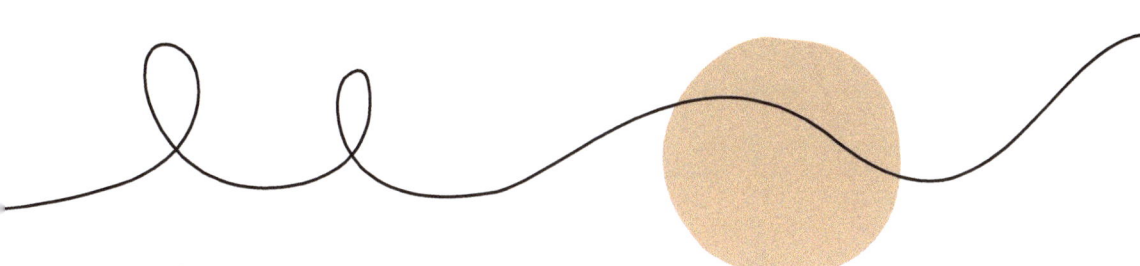

In writing about marri
I had to assess the time in which we
I can not possibly v
about he and
or he and he or she and
I much prefer to write about t
the both of th
the lov
the partr
the people sharing a
may it be a hut or a castle in the clo

they

And so I present to you
A Poem on Marriage
The breath of two people
captured in a timeless hourglass
Each sand going to and fro
Until there is no you and no you
but only us

It is in being us
that partners can hold each other's heart in harmony
Hold hearts
but not hold in cages locked up
Hold means to cherish another's gifts and talents
and help them pursue their dreams
and even those things they never could imagine dreaming of

It is not in the wedding vows
that one repeats in front of God,
or in front of family and friends
that lie the responsibilities
It is in carving of one another's names
in the sand by the sea
each year after year
as a different wave washes it away

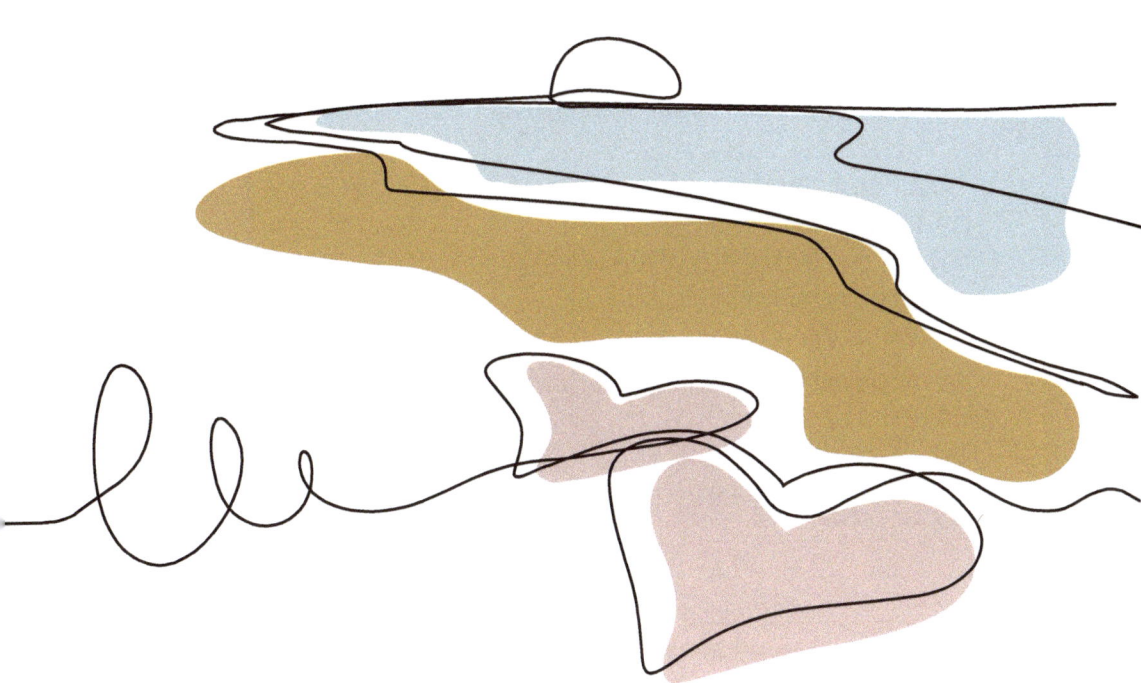

The hour glass has turned
by now decades of times,
the hope is that the wrinkles
on the face are from crying and smiling,
and not so much
from frowning or speaking loudly
Speaking is the key in any relationship,
but hearing the other
is the key that opens all locks

So if you desire to trade a ring circular or cubed
that is fine,
only always remember
that the other has feelings
that are most always more sensitive than yours

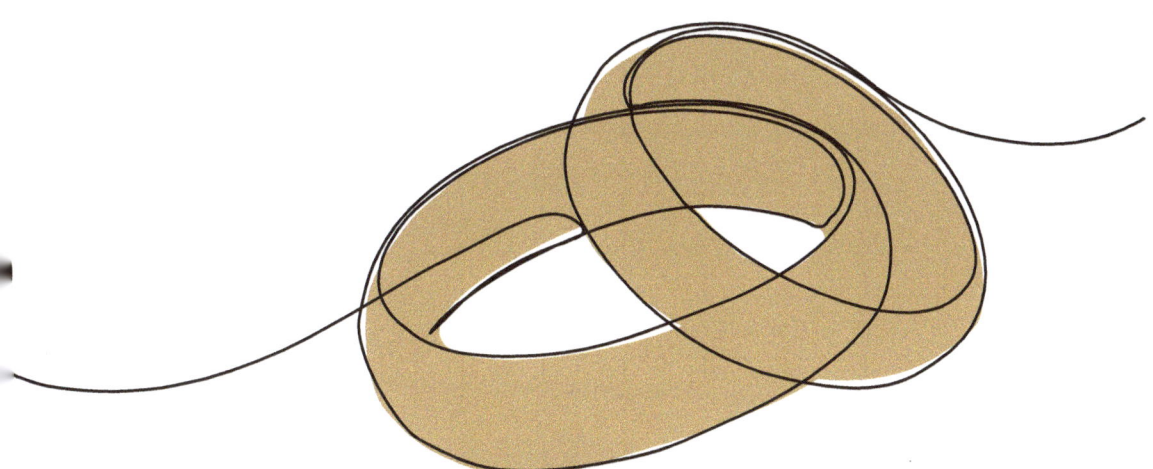

There is a space
which respect and honor
lie in this beautiful relationship,
that space is guarded by rays of light
and it is more fragile than any crystal vase
Hold each others light
in a vase that has a hole at the bottom
Release each others love
so that more may be submitted to light
Fly in each other's shadow
and guidance and honor
one another's voice and wants
Cherish this love
and cherish the light
that surrounds you and you